# RIGHTLY TRAINED

## HOW TO RECOGNIZE A QUALITY SEMINARY EDUCATION

### David K. Spurbeck

**DISPENSATIONAL**
PUBLISHING HOUSE, INC.

Rightly Trained: *How To Recognize A Quality Seminary Education*

Copyright © 2019 David K. Spurbeck
Cover: Leonardo Costa
Cover and Illustrations © 2019 DispensationalPublishing House, Inc.

All rights reserved. This book or any portion thereof may not be reproduced or used in any manner whatsoever without the express written permission of the publisher except for the use of brief quotations in a book review.

Printed in the USA
First Edition, First Printing, 2019
ISBN: 978-1-945774-34-8

DispensationalPublishing House, Inc.
PO Box 3181, Taos, NM 87571

www.dispensationalpublishing.com

Orders by U.S. trade bookstores and wholesalers. Please contact the publisher:
Tel: (844) 321-4202

1 2 3 4 5 6 7 8 9 10

# Table of Contents

Foreword .................................................................. VII

Introduction .............................................................. 1

Some Deficiencies and Suggestions for Contemporary Seminary Programs ..................................................... 5

Changes in Skills ....................................................... 13

Changes in Practice ................................................... 23

Changes in Presentation ............................................ 33

Changes in Ministry .................................................. 43

Conclusion ............................................................... 51

# Foreword

Over 30 years of pastoral ministry, I've become keenly aware that my seminary degree did not prepare me for Biblical ministry. It prepared me for *denominational ministry* and *evangelical ministry*. It prepared me to get "fastest growing church" awards, to build (and pay for) buildings, to operate an efficient church staff, to serve as community liaison, and to repeat what the denominational theologians had produced.

But that, my friends, is a waste of time and money.

When I refer to seminary education, I am referring to a post-graduate ministry degree. The most common (and the "industry standard") is the Master of Divinity (MDiv).

This degree theoretically prepares a young man for an effective pastoral career.

I have become a huge fan of small Bible colleges, which grant undergraduate degrees, and often do a great job at providing the basis for ministry. Many very effective and Biblical preachers have come from Bible colleges. But most men realize the need for more and desire a master's level seminary education. The majority of men in denominational type ministries go through a three-year degree and become "certifiably ready."

There is a huge problem, however. Undergraduate degrees at Bible colleges are limited due to the core requirements of a college level degree. But on the master's level, where a man should become an expert in Greek, Hebrew, exegesis, and hermeneutics, the classroom time is spent in church-growth methods, evangelism methods, administration methods, and denominational histories and agendas. These are things which may have minimal value, but they could be learned by reading a book or listening to a lecture online at one's convenience.

This small book is an attempt to speak to seminaries, seminary students, those wanting to go to seminary, and church members who are typically paying for all of the above. It is time that we begin to demand an academically stringent education that really does make a measurable difference between a Bible college graduate with a bachelor level degree and a seminary graduate with 90-plus hours of "theological" education and a subsequent masters level degree. This book tells what kind of changes should be evident in someone with this degree.

To ever see a change, we will first have to begin to reject "accredited" seminary education. The accreditation process itself is part of the problem, requiring so many courses outside of Biblical languages, theology, and exegesis that there is no time left for that which is most valuable. The accreditation agencies have become promoters of the evangelical church-growth movement, mystic spirituality, and the promulgation of business-world concepts within the church. To be accredited, a seminary is adopting this sociology-based approach. This is one reason why seminaries are notoriously easy academically. The material in the subject matter is self-help, psycho-babble. It is not at all uncommon to hear masters level students talk of how much more challenging their bachelor level work had been. Seminary classes are often nothing more than navel-gazing, philosophical, methodological ponderings. And at average expense of $40,000 per year, they are creating a new generation of pastors that cannot handle the Word of God (let alone rightly divide it) and that is deeply in debt and unable to move to the remote villages of our country (which are so underserved in quality preaching) or to the urban areas (which are perishing because there is no proclamation of God's Word) or to the mission field (which has become a testing ground for social-justice ministries rather than a place of teaching the Word to those who have never heard it).

If you are a seminary president, read this and evaluate your program. If you are a seminary professor, read this and change your subject matter. If you are a Bible college student, read this and choose your seminary carefully and wisely. If you are a pastor, evaluate your own education and the abilities it gave you. You may be like me and decide you will have to self-educate yourself to get the skills that should have been default with a seminary education. If you are a church member, ask questions before you pay for the "preacher boy" to attend the traditional seminary.

Thank you, Dr. David Spurbeck for bringing us these insights. The church desperately needs them.

Randy White,
Dispensational Publishing House, Inc.

# Introduction

A God-honoring seminary education will radically change the student's perspective concerning God and His Word. If the seminary program is what it ought to be, its graduates should expect to see some important results upon graduation. A seminary education should equip a diligent student to be exceptional in his relationship to the Word of God. There should be no comparison between an undergraduate Bible college or Bible institute graduate and a graduate level seminary. A man entering a seminary should expect certain results in practical reality. Unfortunately many seminary programs come up short in some important areas.

The writer is a Bible college graduate who attended college with a number of men who entered the pastorate directly out of college. While circumstance often allow for this, these men lack important instruction that makes one's ministry more effective. Some did go on to seminary yet were not required to study many subjects that provide additional capabilities in communicating and living the Christian life. This does not mean that it is God's will for every pastor-teacher to attend seminary. When the Spirit of God leads a man to seminary, there should be certain core requirements that will give the man equipment to use his pastor-teacher gift more effectively.

Many enter seminary with a set of standards or expectations developed from personal experience in the churches or in their respective colleges. Many college graduates enter seminary with severe limitations in their view of the Scriptures. It is important for them to be aware of their deficiencies that need to be strengthened. After college the writer knew that he was not prepared for the office of bishop (pastor). Many areas of study had been cursory and were often man's opinion or experience rather than God's standards for life and service. Seminary was amazing. Yet even though the training was excellent, after seminary some shortcomings were apparent. This little book is written with the prayer that the apparent shortcomings can be corrected in Seminaries across the land.

# Chapter 1

# Some Deficiencies and Suggestions for Contemporary Seminary Programs

Modern seminary education has added many courses that do not relate to God's program for the church. These classes do little or nothing to give knowledge of God's Word and Scripture-based theology. As a result, many of the classes teach what the professor has done and how he did it. A couple of verses are thrown in to "sanctify" the class. Many seminaries emphasize building experience to qualify the man for a job. Men gather to be trained for an occupation as men do in the world system for any other occupation. These men do not desire to learn the core biblical materials but prefer to learn how to build economically successful churches without a concern for the spiritual growth of the believers. The perspective of the world system has made it expedient to change seminary programs in order to maintain the financial necessities for keeping the doors open. What is the result of these deficiencies? Key courses are eliminated or limited to make room for extraneous classes that often become requirements.

## 1. Deficiencies in Biblical Languages

The first thing to face limitation was the teaching of the biblical languages. Seminaries that required New Testament Greek throughout the program gradually cut back the Greek requirement from every quarter or semester to two years, then to one year, and then to none. Men graduating with degrees from some seminaries have not taken any Greek. This denigrates the degree. Some schools required a year or two of Hebrew. The writer had correspondence from a professor in another seminary in which he bragged about the fact that they required more Hebrew than another seminary in the country for graduation. They required two years, which is less than the three years we require at Dispensational Theological Seminary. Hebrew has been exiled to elective status in most seminaries.

## 2. Deficiencies in Theology

Of all things, theological seminaries have cut back on the requirement of the study of theology. Several core areas of theology that take full quarters for adequate introduction are crammed into single courses. For example Christology, Soteriology, and Pneumatology may be packed into one quarter. Theology proper is just an introduction in classes that include other segments of theology. Many seminary graduates are ignorant of essential areas of theology because they have been deprived by deficient seminary programs. They are novices when they enter ministry. Every hour studying a Bible-based theology will make a man more useful to his God!

## 3. Deficiencies in Biblical Study Courses

Another area of deficiency is the study of the Bible. Many courses are about the Bible but are not really Bible courses. Careful analysis and exegesis is becoming less a part of the programs of many seminaries. Men must master the Bible at least in areas of the New Testament where Christian living is taught. Merely giving the gist of every chapter in the Bible doesn't qualify. Careful attention to details is necessary for one to really understand and compare Scripture with Scripture.

## 4. Deficiencies in Homiletics

Though there is some emphasis on homiletics, many seminary graduates have preached in homiletics classes only once a quarter or semester. There may only be one preaching course required in the seminary program, which is a disservice to the graduate.

One's spiritual gift gives a man a special ability and a greater appetite in the realm of spiritual things. Many seminaries are not designed to teach men with teacher or pastor-teacher gifts. They have gone far away from the original intention of the seminary that was to provide men to fill pulpits in churches. Later other Christian occupations were integrated into seminary programs, thus watering down the original purpose. Ultimately seminaries have been forced to ignore spiritual gifts. Men gifted as pastor-teachers or as teachers need to be teaching men with the same gifts, preparing them for service. They in turn will be involved with the instruction of those with other gifts (*cf.* 2 Tim. 2:2; Eph. 4:11-12). Sadly, many seminaries pay little attention to the New Testament teaching of spiritual gifts.

Seminaries that have compromised on biblical language requirements fail to offer elemental tools for men in their programs who do have teaching gifts. They are instead forced to regurgitate what others have said rather than to herald the Word with authority (1 Tim. 4:2). An extensive knowledge of the biblical languages gives the spiritual pastor-teacher unlimited resources for communicating to believers. It is time for seminaries to resurrect the language requirements. Languages are a challenge to students but the results of diligent study and learning will provide a key for helping Christians grow. Some schools consider the languages to be necessary for a limited number of brilliant students.

Study of biblical languages is not the answer alone. "Junk" courses need to be removed from the curriculum – whether electives or requirements. A graduate student should be able to read books on the subjects of some of these courses and save time for essential courses. The writer enjoys history and enjoyed the history seminary classes he took. He has learned far more by reading histories. The bibliographies from seminary history classes provided resources that expanded knowledge of a multitude of areas of history. Many evangelism classes skip the evangel and teach man's methods.

Theology was once seen as the "queen of the sciences." It should be the queen of every seminary curriculum. Bible-based theology is superior to textbook theology. Inductive study of the theology of Scriptures themselves is essential. Every seminary should require an extensive course in biblical hermeneutics to put curbs on theological studies. Three or four weeks in Christology will never give an accurate view of Jesus Christ!

More exegesis courses are necessary. The professor teaches by his example of sound exegetical method and results. The more of the Bible a seminarian studies in depth the more capable he is in leading God's people. Exegesis and verse-to-verse study provide the spiritual muscle necessary to present the Word of God.

# Chapter 2

# Changes in Skills

A good seminary education should radically change the student's perspective concerning God and His Word. If a seminary program is what it ought to be, its graduates should expect some important results upon graduation if they have adequately worked during their matriculation. Many men enter seminary with a set of standards developed from personal experience in the churches or in their respective colleges. Many Christian college graduates enter seminary with severe limitations in their view of the Scriptures and what they need to know about them. Their study habits should have already been established.

A seminary education should move a man toward Christian maturity and toward mature study habits and skills. Ideally, the years of seminary training should change a man so that he has far greater skills upon graduation than he had when he graduated from college (whether Bible college or not). Some Christian college faculty have recommended that their graduates attend seminary in order to physically and emotionally mature so that churches will consider them as their pastors because they are older. Some have said that their Bible College education was adequate and that they were prepared to accomplish as much as any seminary graduate with their baccalaureate degree. Unfortunately, this may be true when one considers some seminary programs. However, a seminary graduate should show evidence of substantial change since his college training. If not, either he or the seminary has failed. The author believes that the following should be changes that distinguish a seminary graduate from a college graduate. There should be a shift in these skills.

## A. A Shift from the Use of an English Dictionary to a Vast Array of Hebrew, Aramaic and Greek Lexicons

For many years pastors who had not studied at a seminary or had studied at deficient seminaries used the English Bible and an English dictionary for their definitions. Many of their people concluded that Noah Webster and Merriam were among the greatest of theologians in the world because they were quoted so often from the pulpit. These men had never learned that Oxford English Dictionary would give historical word meanings. They thoroughly confused definitions because of the changes in the English language when they used a modern dictionary. Many have found W. E. Vine's Expository Dictionary of New Testament Words too complicated for study. A good seminary education should not only introduce the student to the Hebrew, Aramaic and Greek lexicons but should train the students to use them effectively. Furthermore, a seminary graduate should be equipped to test the definitions of the lexicons by thorough word studies. Such study will produce more accurate and specific definitions from the Scriptures themselves. Too few men were taught in college that the Bible itself provides definitions for words that are God's definitions. Some recognize that Hebrews 11:1 has God's definition of faith. Few know the real definition of praise in Hebrews 13:15 because it is hidden by translation. Therefore an understanding of the Greek is necessary.

A seminary graduate should have seen his professors as good examples in the use of lexical tools. Better yet is a student who jumps beyond the simplistic vocabulary definitions of some lexicons and formulates more precise definitions from the Scriptures themselves.

## B. A Shift from Strong's or Young's Concordances to Hebrew and Greek Concordances

While Strong's and Young's concordances are the bread and butter of English Bible study, other tools are more efficient and accomplish more in less time when one knows the biblical languages and has original language concordances for the Bible. A seminary graduate should at least pick up Englishman's Greek Concordance or Englishman's Hebrew Concordance and use them for study before even bothering with the English concordances. The Plymouth Brethren of the late 19th century are owed a great debt of gratitude for financing and producing these tools (without computers). A seminary graduate should know how to use the indices of these tools to facilitate his studies. Pure language concordances should be a key part of the equipment a seminary graduate has and uses. When a seminary has an adequate language requirement, the language tools are familiar and used for some very specific purposes. In the Old Testament Hebrew-Aramaic concordances include Gerhard Lisowsky's Concordantias Veteris Testamenti and Solomon Mandelkern's Veteris Testamenti Concordantiae that cite every root and list the passages with short citations. More recently Abraham Even-Shoshan's A New Concordance of the Old Testament (2nd ed.) presents the occurrence of every form of every word and its location under all roots. This is an exceptional tool for finding locations of forms in a short Hebrew context.

For the Greek New Testament, W. F. Moulton and A. S. Geden's A Concordance to the Greek Testament remains a standard for finding Greek words in their Greek context. This has been the standard for a hundred years. More recently Philip S. Clapp, Barbara Friberg and Timothy Friberg produced the two-volume Analytical Concordance of the Greek New Testament (1991) that lists forms and identifies them. Their Greek citations of the text are as long as Moulton and Geden and are more specific. Of course there are original language computer programs that provide concordances. The better ones are by Hermeneutica and Gramcord. A consequential problem with these is that in order to see their extent they need to be printed, whereas a book can be seen by the printed page. Some of these tools are completely unfamiliar to college graduates and many seminary graduates.

## C. A Shift from English Commentaries to Hebrew, Aramaic, and Greek Commentaries

Most college graduates have difficulty understanding language commentaries because they do not have adequate training in the biblical languages. A year or two of Greek only makes one dangerous. One need only look at the shelves of the local Christian bookstore to see what is in demand among contemporary pastors. The commentary section is filled with English language froth. Fewer and fewer original language commentaries are being published by Christian publishers (the way things are today, this may be a good thing). Original language commentaries use linguistic terms that are easily understood by the student who has been required to take at least three years of Greek and Hebrew. As a result there is a depth available for his study so that he can accurately represent God. A seminary graduate should produce his own personal commentary on expository series that the Spirit of God leads him to preach.

## D. A Shift from Trusting the Commentaries to Testing the Commentaries

How many men have trusted some commentator only to discover that he held a heresy that was a premise for his commentary? Some of the grand old commentators that many have considered reliable could never have been saved if they believed what their denomination taught about how to be saved. In order to test the commentaries, a seminary graduate should have spent many classroom hours studying a Bible-based theology. Who cares about what Augustus Hopkins Strong says? Men need to know what God says. There isn't enough time to teach enough theology every quarter for three years. Bible college biblical doctrine courses do not equip a man to test the commentaries either from a theological point of view or from a linguistic point of view.

## E. A Shift from Parroting Other Writers or Speakers to Presenting God's Word

One can tell what an untrained man is reading and follows by what and how he teaches and preaches. Ideally, a seminary graduate will go to the Bible from the very beginning of his study and preparation. After he thoroughly exegetes the key passages and has mastered the text, he consults other writers. Usually this means that he has mastered God's Word to the extent that the other writers only make minor contributions if any at all. Careful evaluation of morphology and syntax has already provided more than most writers contribute. The result is that it is God's Word that is presented with confidence rather than a parroting of other men who deserve to get credit for what is said. If a seminary man does not have capabilities in the original languages, he has wasted his time in graduate study. In schools that require adequate language preparation, he has not applied himself, has been lazy, or lacks an aptitude for languages. A person with a pastor-teacher gift has such an appetite for God's Word that diligence in studying the biblical languages is natural. On the other hand, too many institutions barely require enough linguistic study to help the student use the simple language tools. That is the fault of the institution and not the student.

Some may say that these are extremely optimistic, ideal expectations. The fact is that many men are in the office of bishop who are not equipped for preaching and teaching the Word of God even though they have seminary degrees on their walls. Seminary graduates should mature in their ability to prepare for the presentation of the Word and to present it accurately, representing the Chief Shepherd as they "preach the Word" (2 Tim. 2:4)!

# Chapter 3

# Changes in Practice

A seminary education should change not only what a man knows, but also how he knows. His approach to the Scriptures and theology should be very different from those who are not seminary trained. Many men who have attended Christian colleges come out preaching an untested theological system and carry the system to the grave because they learned it from a human mentor or mentors. A seminary graduate should differ from an untrained man in these practices.

## A. A Shift from Accepting a Theological System to Analyzing a Theological System

All students give a measure of credibility to a system of theology that is taught to them by professors they respect. Few learn how to analyze the system for its biblical validity. A seminary graduate should know how to evaluate theological systems because he has been well trained in literal hermeneutics, accurate application, and the Bible as a whole. A logical theological system may be founded on faulty premises that have little or nothing to do with the Scriptures. A good example of this is Reformed theology. A good course in logic will appear to support the system until one examines the premises upon which it is founded. System-oriented persons are among the first to say that it is impossible to take the Bible literally in everything. A seminary graduate should have gained some skills in reading theology critically and in comparing it with the actual revelation of God's Word.

## B. A Shift from Buying a Book-based Theology to Building a Bible-based Theology

A criterion for evaluating the theological position of both Bible college graduates and seminary graduates is the theologies that they studied in school. Professors and schools are identified by the prominent theology studied in the classrooms. Some schools are Berkhof schools, A. H. Strong schools, Chafer schools, and Hodge schools. Graduates from these schools are masters of the theologian and have little or no idea what a Bible-based theology is. Some institutions follow other institutions in a theological system such as Princeton theology or Louisville theology. They follow the structure and accept the conclusions of a specific theologian or theology. A Bible-based theology inductively studies the Bible and derives its theology from the Bible based on the literal interpretation of Scripture. It is far better for a graduate to cite the chapter and verse in the Bible than to cite a page and paragraph in a theology book. Is authority derived from a fallible human theologian or from the infallible Word of God?

## C. A Shift from Believing God Says Something to Knowing Exactly What God Said

How many pastors and professors stand up and preach or teach and say "I believe. . ." when the answer is clearly in Scripture? The exegesis of the passage and comparing Scripture with Scripture actually makes it possible to say, "Thus saith the Lord…" True, there are passages that are not so clear. God said what He said in words in the original languages, and ignorance of the languages prevents a man from really knowing in many areas. Naturally it then becomes necessary in all honesty to say, "I believe." As a result, a man is either a spokesman for God or merely representing himself and his beliefs. This is essential for "cutting the Word of God straight" (2 Tim. 2:15).

## D. A Shift from Subjective, Experience-Based Conclusions to Objective, Bible-Based Conclusions

Experience is the root of theological invention. How many messages are based on an experience that needed a verse to sanctify it in order to teach it or preach it? So often the authority for the application of Scripture of the Word of God is one's personal experience rather than the objective revelation of Scripture. Ideally a seminary will make an effort to avoid the anecdotal approach and teach men to go to the Bible and examine any experiences in light of the literal Word of God for validation. Second Timothy 4:2 says, "Preach the Word," not "Preach your experience." The proliferation of Bible character studies are popular because people identify with their experiences and the story. Twenty weeks studying Joseph is 20 weeks of wasted time for the edification of the believer.

## E. A Shift from Personal, Human Authority in Preaching to Divine Authority in Preaching

Every bit of a pastor's or professor's human, personal authority is of no inherent value. The final authority is the Word of God (2 Tim. 4:2). Real authority must come from the accurate presentation, interpretation and application of the Word of God. A seminary man should be equipped to present the Word of God authoritatively – in its own authority with as little of his authority as possible. A man who attempts to instruct others because of his personal authority prevents the Scriptures from accomplishing what God intended them to accomplish in the lives of the saints.

## F. A Shift from Presenting an Appealing Opinion to Presenting God's Revelation

Colleges and seminaries often have speakers say, "You study the Bible all the time; let me share something practical." The author has heard similar statements in college and seminary chapels many times. Such bad examples leave an imprint on the students who often hear this. Speakers who stand before student gatherings, wave the Bible, and say that they are present to preach the Bible yet never open it but tell their missionary stories, church stories, or experiences create the impression that the institution supports and teaches its students that human opinion is as important as God's revelation. Some schools have a Bible conference which may or may not present the Word of God for a few days and the rest of the time participants are busy with more "practical" programs. This denigrates the divine purpose for biblical revelation.

## G. A Shift from the Priority of English Translations to the Priority of the Original Language Texts

The Authorized King James Version has more tools for studying its text than any other book in the world. Every man in the pulpit should be acquainted with the tools and be using them on a regular basis. One can find anything in the English text with these tools. When a graduate of any institution is English bound, he is forced to rely on the translator. He does not have the ability to check the translation or even evaluate the Authorized Version without a substantial knowledge of the original languages and those texts. Much revelation is concealed in translation. If that is all one has, he is limited in his capability to know what the Spirit of God put in the pages of the Book. The original language text provides the true basis for authoritative preaching (2 Tim. 4:2) and teaching.

## H. A Shift from Making Scriptures Say Something to Accepting What They Actually Say

In order to make a point, some men violate the rules of literal interpretation of Scripture. They will force the passage to say something that it does not say. Ideally a seminary should make such an impression on its men that they are completely filled with the fear of misrepresenting their God and His Word. Presenting the Word of God on a platter without deceit makes it useful for the Spirit of God to use in His teaching ministry in the lives of grace believers (1 Jn. 2:27; Jn. 16:12-13).

## I. A Shift from Contriving Multiple Imaginative Applications of Scripture to Accepting Its Single Application

Much of the application in messages and lessons are no more than pure allegory – reading something into Scripture that is not there. There is only one application for every passage of Scripture unless God clearly gives another. Homiletics is not an excursion into fantasyland.

It should press the student to strive to accurately present God's Word in an unimaginative way without going beyond the normal parameters for the application of God's Word. Misapplication or multiple applications misrepresent the divine intention for the passage. A seminary graduate should have been taught to know better.

These are but a part of the differences that should be evident in a seminary graduate if the seminary is doing its job and the student has taken his training seriously. God will be glorified through His Word without the distraction of His servant.

## Chapter 4

# Changes in Presentation

Ideally a seminary exists to equip men for ministry. The goal is to provide the equipment necessary so that the Spirit of God can efficiently use the man and his spiritual gift to most effectively accomplish the will of God for the man and for other believers. Seminaries frequently have a philosophy of education or ministry which their statement of purpose reflects. Many give written attestation to God and His Word while they require and offer a multitude of courses that do not equip one for ministry. Many of these classes are "how-to" courses that are no more than "how I did it" courses. As an example, the writer has been fascinated by the lack of exegesis and accurate interpretation of Scripture in seminary psychology and counseling classes. Biblical anthropology is barely a subpoint in required theology courses if required at all. The Psalms and the Proverbs have provided the backbone of much that is taught as counsel for Christians. As a result, God the Spirit can do little when the techniques taught are applied in ministry and all that happens is that carnal believers function in different and more acceptable works of the flesh. When seminaries require such courses, they prevent the student from taking adequate Bible courses, theology courses, and biblical language courses. Ideally a seminary graduate should have graduated from a level of mediocrity to a level of proficiency because the Spirit has led him to a seminary where that is possible. A potential seminarian should anticipate these personal changes in biblical presentation.

## A. A Shift from a Focus on the Messenger to a Focus on the Message

College mentality is that a man be presented in the best light in order to attract the listener to him and his mechanisms for communication. If the man looks good, sounds good, and has good stories and jokes, then he is a good speaker. The message becomes secondary to the speaker's presence and presentation. In order for this to happen, the real truth of the Bible is diluted when used. A seminary graduate should know the Bible so well that its inherent qualities press him to present it and its message rather than himself.

## B. A Shift from a Message of Human Origin to a Message of Divine Origin

Structure is great as long as it accurately represents the Word of God. A seminary graduate should never need to use the popular sermon services available in books, through the mail and on the Internet. It is embarrassing when one thinks of how many times the sermons in Handfuls on Purpose have been preached as the Word of God over the last century. These sets and services tend to be diving boards for preachers. They provide a platform to dive from a passage of Scripture into any subject that has entered the mind of the writer and the reader. As a result, many of these men hastily depart from the text and rarely return to it, except in the conclusion to sanctify the subject preached with a biblical "stamp of approval." Biblical exposition is founded on biblical exegesis. Exposition takes the results of exegesis and presents it in language that the people can understand without compromising the actual meaning of the text. It is the Word of God that "is profitable for doctrine to be believed but not practiced, for reproof, for correction, for child training in righteousness so that a man belonging to God may be well-rounded {and not lopsided} having been thoroughly well rounded for every good work" (my translation of 2 Tim. 3:16-17). A man may give good human advice, but the responsibility of a pastor-teacher is to present God's Word. When a man is consistent in preaching the Word of God, Christians who hear him teach and preach will be meeting with God through His Word rather than meeting with the man through his words.

## C. A Shift from Accepting the Latest Theological Fads to Knowing the Theology of the Bible

A visit to the local Christian bookstore exposes one to a multitude of theological fads. Piles of books that are filled with heresy are featured. Many of these are merely new spins on old heresies in the modern environment of Christendom. Unfortunately seminaries are squeezing out systematic theology courses and replacing them with theological faddism in "junk" courses. A seminary graduate should know how to dig theology out of the Bible rather than to buy the latest fad. Effective, extensive training in a Bible-based theology provides the basis for a man to be a true spokesman for God and who accurately represents God. The man needs to know the theology and to have the linguistic capabilities to discover that theology in the pages of Scripture rightly divided. Not many doctrines in Scripture are taught in a single verse. A comparison of multiple passages is necessary to understand the substance of most of the teaching in the Bible. Many of the fads take a single verse out of the text without studying the whole of revelation on the subject, thereby producing flawed teaching and popular heresy.

## D. A Shift from English Grammar to Hebrew, Aramaic and Greek Grammar

While English grammar does provide some insight in most English translations, it is not precise enough to expose the intricacies of the text of the Scriptures in the original languages. Few languages are as precise as the Greek language. The whole spectrum of the Greek verb opens divine revelation for understanding. While Hebrew and Aramaic are less complicated than Greek, they have a special system of verb stems that is difficult to see in an English text. These languages bring the student closer to the words of God in the text than English does. There is a broad line between the seminaries that require only two years of Greek and a year of Hebrew and those that require an adequate program for the exegesis of the Word of God. Limited training gives students a false security concerning their ability to exegete the text. This is dangerous because those students who have not mastered the grammar and language will misrepresent the Scriptures while claiming that their authority is in the languages. A minimum of four years of Greek and three years of Hebrew is necessary to have adequate knowledge for preaching the Word of God from the original languages.

## E. A Shift from Sloppy Human Interpretation to a Strict Literal Interpretation

When a person who is a student of the Scriptures enters a preaching or teaching situation, he will quickly detect how the Scriptures are handled. Characteristic of the untrained preacher or teacher is careless or sloppy interpretation of Scripture. One stops and says, "But it doesn't say that! Where did you get that?" The interpretation could have come from anywhere, but it certainly didn't come from God and His Word. Few Bible colleges require a course in hermeneutics (the science of Bible interpretation). They may offer courses on Bible study methods, including how to find principles in the Bible and how to live and apply the Bible. The time has come when seminaries no longer require hermeneutics classes. Many feel that a consistent hermeneutic limits what a preacher or teacher can do with the Word of God, that the literal interpretation of Scripture is confining, and that it places limits on the preacher and teacher. However, consistent literal interpretation permits a preacher or teacher to represent God and His Word accurately. A consistent literal interpretation and its consistent single application permit the Holy Spirit to illumine the spiritual believer to know God's thoughts as they are presented in the Scriptures.

## F. A Shift from Multiple Translations to a Literal Core of Translation Based on the Text

Many pastors are collectors of English translations because these are the only resources they have for preaching due to their limited original language ability. A seminary graduate may have a collection of translations for several reasons, but his own translation of the Word of God is his first responsibility. Bible translation immerses one into the Word of God. Comparing translations creates confusion unless one can evaluate them critically from the text of the original languages. Much time is wasted in comparing translations without going to the text first and applying the rules of morphology and syntax to understand the text. More often than not the inaccuracies of the translations demonstrate that the use of some versions will not edify believers. Recently the author prepared messages using five different versions because he did not know which versions the people would be using. Once again it was eye-opening to see how some important Christian-life issues had been concealed by translators because of their theology. Real sermon preparation is not spreading ten versions out on the floor and trying to find the ones a person likes best to preach a passage. A carnal pastor may choose the wrong translation and preach it as the Word of God.

A pastor-teacher needs to be adequately equipped and know the Word of God so well that he can communicate it to a seven-year-old as well as a 70-year-old with a PhD. How can "missionaries" teach aboriginals the Word without adequate equipment to put the Word of God on their level? A goal of a good seminary program is to provide the tools that equip the man for reaching any level. It is more difficult to communicate the Word of God to youngsters and the less-educated than most think. Ignorance need not breed ignorance, especially in spiritual matters. In some instances it takes a seminary education to teach a child certain truths and to be responsive to his questions and uncertainties. We do not give the Greek to a seven-year-old, but what we tell him should accurately reflect the meaning of the passage because it may stay with him for the rest of him life.

## Chapter 5

# Changes in Ministry

After teaching at the seminary level for more than 40 years and attending seminary for more than five years and being a pastor for almost 50 years, the author sees these as ideals for one who graduates from seminary. These ideals may seem too strong and even narrow-minded. However, God raised up seminaries to train and equip men to meet His standards for His flock. Seminary graduation should make a difference and distinguish the graduate from the masses in ministry. The church should expect more from seminary graduates. The church has the right to expect the seminary graduate to know the Bible, to know how to study the Bible, to know and use the original languages of the Bible, to have a thorough knowledge of the core of a Bible-based theology, to know how to communicate the Word of God, to know how to live the Christian life, and to actually be living it. A four-year Bible college program only begins to provide adequate instruction especially with all of the government's degree requirements. Unfortunately some men go to seminary and graduate without being required to take courses that will adequately prepare them to do God's work with His Word. Too many hours in many seminaries are spent teaching men about everything under the sun except the Bible, its languages and its theology. The author often looks at these programs as did a preacher from antiquity who wrote: *"Emptiness of emptinesses, says the Preacher, emptiness of emptinesses, the whole thing is emptiness . . . The whole thing is emptiness and striving after wind"* (Eccl. 1:2,14; 12:8 – author's translation). Ideally a seminary education should change a man's ministry in these ways.

## A. A Shift from Developing Human Inconsistencies to Depending on Divine Consistency

A professor made this statement during the author's first-quarter seminary theology course: "O, the blessedness of consistency!" Mankind is prone to inconsistency. Pastors are leaders who pass their inconsistencies on to future generations in the church. Human inconsistencies are subjective responses to the text of Scripture. God is always consistent. When Scripture is interpreted literally, God's consistency is evident. When a man teaches Old Testament as doctrine for Christian practice, there is an immediate confrontation with God's consistency. God deals with different men at different times in different ways with different results. A seminary's goal should be the same as Paul had for Timothy. *"Be eager to present* (because it is His right by purchase) *yourself as an approved one to God, a workman that is unashamed, continually cutting straight the word of the truth* (2 Tim. 2:15)." Cutting straight or rightly dividing the Word of God presents a divine consistency. When men are trained and permitted to misapply Scripture and to modify literal interpretation, they can lead their people to shipwreck their faith (*cf.* Hymenaeus and Alexander in 1Tim. 1:18-20). Divine consistency provides divinely provided revelation that should produce a God-glorifying spiritual life.

## B. A Shift from a "Philosophy of Ministry" to the Simplicity of Grace Revelation and God's Arrangement for Ministry

The idea of a "philosophy of ministry" is not just perpetuated in undergraduate Christian institutions but also in seminaries. Grace revelation provides more than adequate information as to how God expects the local church to accomplish His program. The idea of a "philosophy of ministry" is most often an excuse for putting human ideas to the test in a local church. It is the world system infiltrating the church. God's program does not manipulate souls to bring them in and to keep them in the church. It is designed to relate to the human spirit of saints – the realm of their salvation – so that they can function in their present-tense salvation. A seminary graduate should have a thorough comprehension of present-tense salvation and relate to God's program for maturing saints in present-tense salvation. God's arrangements for ministry are based on this. This is the reason for the existence of the Church which is His Body (Eph. 1:22-23).

## C. A Shift from Human Methodology of the World System to God's Infallible Methodology

The church is not a business, educational institution, entertainment entity or social club. Many courses in church administration, evangelism, church operations and missions do no more than bring the methods of the world system into the local church. This is not a proper use of the world system but rather the abuse of it (*cf.* 1 Cor. 7:31). The world system creates complexity with minimal accountability. God has provided a system of simple methods that bring Him glory and that are built on the spiritual life and the inherent responsibility of grace believers to the Father through the Spirit. God's methods do not produce bigger churches and ecclesiastical bureaucracy but are designed to bring glory to God alone.

## D. A Shift from "How I Did It" to "How God Gets It Done"

Somewhere and in some way seminary training must clarify the origin of the good works for the believer. How often do those who earn graduate degrees hold themselves in high esteem because of the possession of the degree and the accomplishments that led to it? The degree only indicates a level of preparation for one to do the good works that God has prepared for him. *"For we are a product* [the result of His doing], *having been created in Christ Jesus unto a good quality of works, which were prepared beforehand, in order that we might order the details of our lives in them* [the good works]" (Eph. 2:10). When the Holy Spirit leads a man to seminary, He leads so that the man can use his spiritual gift and provide a means for the Spirit to minister. A characteristic of many traditional seminary chapels was the speaker who told men how he did things. The author heard one man say that he was not going to speak from the Bible but wanted to address "practical things." These proved to be how he engaged in "successful" church ministry. It became evident that God had done nothing and that the success was world-system success accompanied by a great harvest of tares. A seminary man needs to learn that God does His work through a spiritual man; otherwise the work is that of mere man. Seminaries without an accurate spiritual life course will never produce such men, nor do they have the potential to do so.

## E. A Shift from "I Know" to "I Know That I Don't Know"

Many believe that a seminary degree makes them instant authorities concerning theology and the Word of God. As a result, human authority replaces divine authority. The more one knows about the Bible the more he knows that he does not know about it. That is the way that the Word of God is written. The Bible is inexhaustible as a source of divine information. For example a student can study Greek and know that the preposition εν (*en*) can occur as locative "in" or instrumental "by." The context in which the preposition is found should determine how one translates the form. In a number of places one can interpret the context in either way. "I know that I don't know which it is, though I may have a preference." The more one studies the Bible the greater the foundation upon which the Divine Teacher, the Holy Spirit, can build. A seminary education should provide a substantial foundation for further, extensive study of the Scriptures in cooperation with the Holy Spirit. A seminary graduate must not be a know-it-all but must understand that there is much more to learn. He must see His future as one of learning about his God and His program for the rest of his life, knowing that there is much more to know.

This is a perspective of what a seminary education should be. Today many seminaries have ignored God and His Word in their programs. Men graduate with a multitude of classes that are impractically "practical." Standards are compromised. Students are misdirected. Man gets glory. God is secondary. Students are not motivated to mature. The seriousness of the training is denigrated in practice. If a seminary does not offer a program that will distinguish a graduate from other men with other training, it is a failure. If a man does not graduate with these distinguishing features, either he did not apply himself adequately or the program was nonproductive. May each one be prepared to divide the Word of God rightly and to live a spiritual life toward maturity.

# Conclusion

We began this little book by stating that, "A man entering seminary should expect certain results in practical reality." Throughout the book, we showed a glimpse of what this practical reality should be. Seminaries are almost always showing deficiencies in biblical languages, theology, biblical studies, and homiletics. They are not helping young men who are preparing for ministry change their skill levels beyond what a Bible college education itself provides (or a good layman's study course, for that matter). We have stated that the seminary graduate should be skilled at the usage of a vast array of Biblical language lexicons, concordances, and commentaries. In addition, he should have made a shift from *trusting* the commentaries to *testing* the commentaries and from *parroting* other writers to *presenting* God's Word. The seminary graduate should have also made a shift from *accepting* a theological system to *analyzing* theological systems. He should have begun the development of a Bible-based theology rather than buying his theology from popular books. Perhaps most importantly, the seminary graduate should shift from subjective, experience-based conclusions to objective, Bible-based conclusions. This, in itself, will keep the pastor from making Scriptures say something rather than accepting what Scriptures say!

The author prays for the day when the focus of the ministry is the *message* and not the *messenger*. Will the day come when it is standard practice that the theology of the Bible overturns the latest theological fads? If this happens, a Divine consistency will be displayed in preaching and ministry, one that is sorely needed today. We need to quit focusing on philosophy of ministry and begin focusing on the simplicity of grace and God's arrangement for ministry.

Will you pray with us that this little booklet can help pastors become "rightly trained?"

**Dispensational Publishing House** is striving to become the go-to source for Bible-based materials from the dispensational perspective.

Our goal is to provide high-quality doctrinal and worldview resources that make dispensational theology accessible to people at all levels of understanding.

Visit our blog regularly to read informative articles from both known and new writers.

And please let us know how we can better serve you.

Dispensational Publishing House, Inc.
PO Box 3181
Taos, NM 87571

Call us toll free 844-321-4202

www.DispensationalPublishing.com

www.ingramcontent.com/pod-product-compliance
Lightning Source LLC
Chambersburg PA
CBHW052207110526
44591CB00012B/2113